Pro-Wrestling Superstar
John Cena

by Jon M. Fishman

BUMBA BOOKS™

LERNER PUBLICATIONS ◆ MINNEAPOLIS

Note to Educators

Throughout this book, you'll find critical-thinking questions. These can be used to engage young readers in thinking critically about the topic and in using the text and photos to do so.

Lerner Publications Company
A division of Lerner Publishing Group, Inc.
241 First Avenue North
Minneapolis, MN 55401 USA

For reading levels and more information, look up this title at www.lernerbooks.com.

Main body text set in Helvetica Textbook Com Roman 23/49.
Typeface provided by Linotype AG.

Library of Congress Cataloging-in-Publication Data

The Cataloging-in-Publication Data for *Pro-Wrestling Superstar John Cena* is on file at the Library of Congress.
ISBN 978-1-5415-5565-5 (lib. bdg.)
ISBN 978-1-5415-7363-5 (pbk.)
ISBN 978-1-5415-5655-3 (eb pdf)

Manufactured in the United States of America
1-46020-42937-11/8/2018

Table of
Contents

Strong Man

John Cena crashes into another wrestler.

Smash! John is a wrestling superstar.

John grew up with

four brothers.

They loved to wrestle

one another.

John lifted weights in high school.

He grew big and strong.

Why do people try to get stronger?

John liked other sports too.

He played football in college.

Why do people go to college?

John became a pro wrestler after college.

Then he joined the WWE.

John was a great wrestler.

People loved to watch

him wrestle.

John won many matches.

He became a WWE

champion.

Wrestling made John famous.

He starred in movies and TV shows.

John works hard at wrestling.

He wants to be a

pro-wrestling superstar

for a long time!

Pro-Wrestling Gear

mat

ropes

shoes

shorts

Picture Glossary

champion

winner of the top prize

college

school after high school

matches

wrestling contests

WWE

a pro-wrestling group

Read More

Kortemeier, Todd. *Superstars of WWE*. Mankato, MN: Amicus, 2017.

Pantaleo, Steve. *How to Be a WWE Superstar*. New York: DK, 2017.

Rebman, Nick. *Wrestling*. Lake Elmo, MN: Focus Readers, 2019.

Index

Photo Credits

Image credits: STRINGER/AFP/Getty Images, pp. 5, 20, 23 (bottom right); AP Photo/Jonathan Bachman, pp. 7, 23 (top right); Kristian Dowling/Getty Images, p. 8; Courtesy of Springfield College, Babson Library, Archives and Special Collections, pp. 11, 23 (bottom left); Don Arnold/WireImage/Getty Images, p. 12; Moses Robinson/Getty Images, p. 15; Suzanne Cordeiro/Corbis/Getty Images, pp. 17, 23 (top left); RGR Collection/Alamy Stock Photo, p. 18; Gearstd/iStock/Getty Images, p. 22 (top); Vladyslav Starozhylov/Shutterstock.com, p. 22 (bottom left); herreid/iStock/Getty Images, p. 22 (bottom right).

Cover: TIZIANA FABI/AFP/Getty Images.